EDITED BY
PIETRO PRINCIPE

TRANSLATED BY
JOSEPH MURPHY

Artwork
Gian Carlo Olcuire

One of the risen holds out a Rosary to two companions, enabling them to climb into Paradise

Michelangelo Buonarroti, **Last Judgment** *(detail)*, 1536-41

Plan

Blessed Fra Angelico, *Madonna and Child*, c. 1435

Introduction

The Rosary or "crown of roses" is a prayerful reflection on the life of Jesus, which involves contemplating certain Gospel scenes, the "mysteries", in the company of Mary. "To recite the Rosary is nothing other than to contemplate with Mary the face of Christ." [1]

For centuries, this has been a prayer "loved by countless Saints and encouraged by the Magisterium". [2]

Many are the events connected with the Blessed Virgin Mary in which she encourages people to say the Rosary. All are free to avail themselves of the message of these events.

The meditations in this booklet are based on Sacred Scripture, the Catechism of the Catholic Church and Pope John Paul II 's Apostolic Letter on the Rosary.

This approach ensures fidelity to the deposit of Faith.

Pope John Paul II has supplemented the Christological dimension of the Rosary by adding the "mysteries of light", which are based on certain episodes of the public ministry of Christ.

For this reason it can truly be said that the Rosary is a "summary of the Gospel".

---

[1] Apostolic Letter *Rosarium Virginis Mariae*, 3, henceforth abbreviated as R.V.M.

[2] R.V.M., 1.

What kind of prayer is the Rosary?

In his Apostolic Letter *Rosarium Virginis Mariae*, Pope John Paul II writes: "The Rosary, precisely because it starts with Mary's own experience, is *an exquisitely contemplative prayer*. Without this contemplative dimension, it would lose its meaning, as Pope Paul VI clearly pointed out: 'Without contemplation, the Rosary is a body without a soul, and its recitation runs the risk of becoming a mechanical repetition of formulas'."[3]

The Rosary, which is based on repetition, presupposes a lively faith and sincere love of Christ the Redeemer and the Virgin Mary.

"In effect, the Rosary is simply *a method of contemplation*. As a method, it serves as a means to an end and cannot become an end in itself. All the same, as the fruit of centuries of experience, this method should not be undervalued. In its favour one could cite the experience of countless Saints."[4]

---

[3] R.V.M., 12.
[4] R.V.M., 28.

Gian Lorenzo Bernini, *Baldacchino* (detail), Rome, St Peter's Basilica, 1624-32

The Rosary beads

"The traditional aid used for the recitation of the Rosary is the set of beads. At the most superficial level, the beads often become a simple counting mechanism to mark the succession of *Hail Marys*."[5]

"It is quite another thing, however, when the Rosary is thought of as an outpouring of that love which tirelessly returns to the person loved with expressions similar in their content but ever fresh in terms of the feeling pervading them."[6]

"Here the first thing to note is the way *the beads converge upon the Crucifix*, which both opens and closes the unfolding

sequence of prayer. The life and prayer of believers is centred upon Christ."[7]

[5] R.V.M., 36.
[6] R.V.M., 26.
[7] R.V.M., 36.

The history of the Rosary

"The Rosary was part of the great flourishing of new forms of devotion to the Blessed Virgin in its more popular aspects, which marked the end of the 12th century. The Cistercians and, from the beginning of the next century, the great mendicant Orders, in their determined struggle against heresy, contributed in no small way to its spread. … The Rosary beads, already in use for similar devotions, were adopted to ensure easier and more attentive recitation. Very soon mention of the mysteries of the life of Jesus and Mary was introduced into this recitation. … St Dominic and his friars in their mission of preaching to the people were very much part of this movement, but it is not easy to determine the precise form they practised and spread. A kind of official approval was granted when St Pius V laid down a fixed and uniform text for the *Hail Mary*."[8]

---

[8] *Enciclopedia Cattolica*, Vol. X, p. 1350.

At both Lourdes and Fatima the Virgin Mary encouraged people to pray the Rosary.[9]

During the Second Millennium many Popes encouraged Marian devotion, and since the time of Leo XIII, the "Pope of the Rosary", all of them have recommended this prayer and enriched it by attaching indulgences to its recitation.

Pope John Paul II has always had a special devotion to the Mother of God. His coat of arms bears the first words (*Totus tuus*) of an invocation to the Virgin Mary. He

always has a Rosary with him and continually recites it. The Apostolic Letter on the Rosary is a permanent reminder of his high esteem for this prayer.

[9] Cf. R.V.M., 7.

How to pray the Rosary

"At present, in different parts of the Church, there are many ways to introduce the Rosary".[10]

One of the ways is the following.

Begin by making the Sign of the Cross, saying:

In the name of the Father and of the Son and of the Holy Spirit.

O God come to my aid;

O Lord, make haste to help me.

Glory be to the Father, and to the Son, and to the Holy Spirit.

As it was in the beginning, is now, and ever shall be, world without end. Amen.

At the beginning of each decade, announce the "mystery" to be contemplated, for example, the first joyful mystery is "The Annunciation".

After a short pause for reflection, recite the "Our Father", ten "Hail Marys" and the "Glory be to the Father".

An invocation may be added after each decade.

At the end of the Rosary, the Loreto Litany or some other Marian prayer is recited.

[10] R.V.M., 37.

Sassoferrato, *Madonna and Child*, c. 1650

The Mysteries of the Rosary

The Rosary is made up of twenty "mysteries" (significant events or moments in the life of Jesus and Mary), which, following the Apostolic Letter *Rosarium Virginis Mariae*, are grouped into four series.

The first contains the **joyful mysteries** (recited on Mondays and Saturdays); the second, the **mysteries of light** (Thursdays); the third, the **sorrowful mysteries** (Tuesdays and Fridays); and the fourth, the **glorious mysteries** (Wednesdays and Sundays).

"This indication is not intended to limit a rightful freedom in personal and community prayer, where account needs to be taken of spiritual and pastoral needs and of the occurrence of particular liturgical celebrations which might call for suitable adaptations."[11]

As an aid to the meditative and contemplative journey of the Rosary, two texts are given for each 'mystery': one from Sacred Scripture, the other from the Catechism of the Catholic Church.

A work of art helps us fix our mind on the mystery.

[11] R.V.M., 38.

Masolino, *The Annunciation*, 1425-30

THE ANNUNCIATION

"In the sixth month the angel Gabriel was sent from God to a city of Galilee named Nazareth, to a virgin betrothed to a man whose name was Joseph, of the house of David; and the virgin's name was Mary" (*Lk* 1:26-27).

"The Annunciation to Mary inaugurates the 'fullness of time' (*Gal* 4:4), the time of the fulfilment of God's promises and preparations" (*CCC*, 484).

The Visitation, Salerno, Diocesan Museum, 11th century ivory

THE VISITATION

"In those days Mary arose and went with haste into the hill country, to a city of Judah, and she entered the house of Zechariah and greeted Elizabeth. And when Elizabeth heard the greeting of Mary, the babe leaped in her womb; and Elizabeth was filled with the Holy Spirit and she exclaimed with a loud cry, 'Blessed are you among women, and blessed is the fruit of your womb!'" (*Lk* 1:39-42).

"Mary's visitation to Elizabeth thus became a visit from God to his people" (*CCC*, 717).

Giotto, *The Nativity*, 1305-06

THE BIRTH OF OUR LORD

"In those days a decree went out from Caesar Augustus that all the world should be enrolled. This was the first enrolment, when Quirinius was governor of Syria. And all went to be enrolled, each to his own city.

And Joseph also went up from Galilee, from the city of Nazareth, to Judea, to the city of David, which is called Bethlehem, because he was of the house and lineage of David, to be enrolled with Mary, his betrothed, who was with child. And while they were there, the time came for her to be delivered.

And she gave birth to her first-born son and wrapped him in swaddling cloths, and laid him in a manger, because there was no place for them in the inn" (*Lk* 2:1-7).

"Jesus was born in a humble stable, into a poor family. Simple shepherds were the first witnesses to this event. In this poverty heaven's glory was made manifest" (*CCC*, 525).

Giotto, *The Presentation in the Temple*, 1320-25

THE PRESENTATION IN THE TEMPLE

"And at the end of eight days, when he was circumcised, he was called Jesus, the name given by the angel before he was conceived in the womb. And when the time came for their purification according to the law of Moses, they brought him up to Jerusalem to present him to the Lord (as it is written in the law of the Lord, *'Every male that opens the womb shall be called holy to the Lord'*) and to offer a sacrifice according to what is said in the law of the Lord, *'a pair of turtledoves, or two young pigeons'*" (Lk 2:21-24).

"Jesus' circumcision, on the eighth day after his birth, is the sign of his incorporation into Abraham's descendants, into the people of the covenant. It is the sign of his submission to the Law" (*CCC*, 527).

Simone Martini, *The Holy Family after the Finding of Jesus in the Temple*, first half of the 14th century

THE FINDING OF JESUS
IN THE TEMPLE

"**N**ow his parents went to Jerusalem every year at the feast of the Passover. And when he was twelve years old, they went up according to custom; and when the feast was ended, as they were returning, the boy Jesus stayed behind in Jerusalem. His parents did not know it ...
After three days they found him in the temple, sitting among the teachers, listening to them and asking them questions; and all who heard him were amazed at his understanding and his answers" (*Lk* 2:41-47).

"**T**he *finding of Jesus in the temple* is the only event that breaks the silence of the Gospels about the hidden years of Jesus. Here Jesus lets us catch a glimpse of the mystery of his total consecration to a mission that flows from his divine sonship: 'Did you not know that I must be about my Father's work?' (*Lk* 2:49)" (*CCC*, 534).

Andrea Verrocchio and Leonardo da Vinci, *The Baptism of Jesus*, c. 1475

THE BAPTISM
IN THE JORDAN

"**A**nd when Jesus was baptized, he went up immediately from the water, and behold, the heavens were opened and he saw the Spirit of God descending like a dove, and alighting on him; and lo, a voice from heaven, saying, 'This is my beloved Son, with whom I am well pleased'" (*Mt* 3:16-17).

"Jesus' public life begins with his baptism by John in the Jordan. John preaches 'a baptism of repentance for the forgiveness of sins' (*Lk* 3:3)" (*CCC*, 535).

Duccio, *The Wedding Feast of Cana*, 1308-11

The wedding feast of Cana

"On the third day there was a marriage at Cana in Galilee, and the mother of Jesus was there; Jesus also was invited to the marriage, with his disciples. When the wine failed, the mother of Jesus said to him, 'They have no wine.' And Jesus said to her, 'O woman, what have you to do with me? My hour has not yet come.' His mother said to the servants, 'Do whatever he tells you'" (*Jn* 2:1-5).

"On the threshold of his public life Jesus performs his first sign – at his mother's request – during a wedding feast. The Church attaches great importance to Jesus' presence at the wedding at Cana. She sees in it the confirmation of the goodness of marriage and the proclamation that thenceforth marriage will be an efficacious sign of Christ's presence" (*CCC*, 1613).

Blessed Fra Angelico, *The Sermon on the Mount*, 1440-52

THE PROCLAMATION OF THE KINGDOM OF GOD

"The time is fulfilled, and the kingdom of God is at hand; repent, and believe in the gospel" (*Mk* 1:15).

"*Everyone* is called to enter the Kingdom. First announced to the children of Israel, this messianic kingdom is intended to accept men of all nations" (*CCC*, 543).

Raffaelo Sanzio, *The Transfiguration*, 1518-20

The transfiguration

"**A**nd after six days Jesus took with him Peter and James and John his brother, and led them up a high mountain apart. And he was transfigured before them, and his face shone like the sun, and his garments became white as light" (*Mt* 17:1-2).

"**F**or a moment Jesus discloses his divine glory, confirming Peter's confession. He also reveals that he will have to go by the way of the cross at Jerusalem in order to 'enter into his glory' (*Lk* 24:26)" (*CCC*, 555).

Blessed Fra Angelico and his school, *The Eucharist*, 1438-42

"Now as they were eating, Jesus took bread, and blessed, and broke it, and gave it to the disciples and said, 'Take, eat; this is my body'" (*Mt* 26:26).

"By celebrating the Last Supper with his Apostles in the course of the Passover meal, Jesus gave the Jewish Passover its definitive meaning. Jesus' passing over to his Father by his Death and Resurrection, the new Passover, is anticipated in the Supper and celebrated in the Eucharist, which fulfils the Jewish Passover and anticipates the final Passover of the Church in the glory of the Kingdom" (*CCC*, 1340).

Blessed Fra Angelico, *Prayer of Jesus in the Garden*, first half of the 15th century

The agony in the garden

"Then Jesus went with them to a place called Gethsemane, and he said to his disciples, 'Sit here, while I go yonder and pray.' And taking with him Peter and the two sons of Zebedee, he began to be sorrowful and troubled. Then he said to them, 'My soul is very sorrowful, even to death; remain here, and watch with me.' And going a little farther he fell on his face and prayed, 'My Father, if it be possible, let this cup pass from me; nevertheless, not as I will, but as you will'" (*Mt* 26:36-39).

"Such a battle and such a victory become possible only through prayer. It is by his prayer that Jesus vanquishes the Tempter, both at the outset of his public mission and in the ultimate struggle of his agony" (*CCC*, 2849).

Blessed Fra Angelico, *The Mocking of Christ*, 1440-52

"Then Pilate took Jesus and scourged him. And the soldiers plaited a crown of thorns, and put it on his head, and arrayed him in a purple robe; they came up to him, saying, 'Hail, King of the Jews!' and struck him with their hands" (*Jn* 19:1-3).

"Jesus' sufferings took their historical, concrete form from the fact that he was 'rejected by the elders and the chief priests and the scribes' (*Mk* 8:31), who 'handed him to the Gentiles to be mocked and scourged and crucified' (*Mt* 20:19)" (*CCC*, 572).

Antonello da Messina, *The Mocking of Christ*, 15th century

THE CROWNING WITH THORNS

"Then the soldiers of the governor took Jesus into the praetorium, and they gathered the whole battalion before him. And they stripped him and put a scarlet robe upon him, and plaiting a crown of thorns they put it on his head, and put a reed in his right hand. And kneeling before him they mocked him, saying, 'Hail, King of the Jews!'" (*Mt* 27:27-29).

"It is love 'to the end' (*Jn* 13:1) that confers on Christ's sacrifice its value as redemption and reparation, as atonement and satisfaction. He knew and loved us all when he offered his life" (*CCC*, 616).

Hieronymus Bosch, *Christ carries the Cross*, 1515-16

THE CARRYING
OF THE CROSS

"And they compelled a passer-by, Simon of Cyrene, who was coming in from the country, the father of Alexander and Rufus, to carry his cross. And they brought him to the place called Golgotha (which means the place of a skull)" (*Mk* 15:21-22).

"By accepting in his human will that the Father's will be done, he accepts his death as redemptive, for 'he himself bore our sins in his body on the tree' (*1 Pt* 2:24)" (*CCC*, 612).

Masaccio, *The Crucifixion*, 1426

"**A**nd when they came to the place which is called The Skull, there they crucified him, and the criminals, one on the right and one on the left. And Jesus said, 'Father, forgive them; for they know not what they do' ...

It was now about the sixth hour, and there was darkness over the whole land until the ninth hour, while the sun's light failed; and the curtain of the temple was torn in two. Then Jesus, crying with a loud voice, said, 'Father, into thy hands I commit my spirit!' And having said this he breathed his last" (*Lk* 23:33-46).

"'**C**hrist died for our sins in accordance with the scriptures' (*1 Cor* 15:3)" (*CCC*, 619).

Matthias Grünewald, *The Resurrection*, 1513-15

THE RESURRECTION

"But on the first day of the week, at early dawn, they went to the tomb, taking the spices which they had prepared. And they found the stone rolled away from the tomb, but when they went in they did not find the body. While they were perplexed about this, behold, two men stood by them in dazzling apparel; and as they were frightened and bowed their faces to the ground, the men said to them, 'Why do you seek the living among the dead? He is not here, but has risen'" (*Lk* 24:1-5).

"'If Christ has not been raised, then our preaching is in vain and your faith is in vain' (*1 Cor* 15:14). The Resurrection above all constitutes the confirmation of all Christ's works and teachings" (*CCC*, 651).

Andrea Mantegna, *The Ascension*, 1460

THE ASCENSION

"**S**o then the Lord Jesus, after he had spoken to them, was taken up into heaven, and sat down at the right hand of God" (*Mk* 16:19).

"**T**his final stage stays closely linked to the first, that is, to his descent from heaven in the Incarnation. Only the one who 'came from the Father' can return to the Father: Christ Jesus" (*CCC*, 661).

Tiziano Vecellio, *Pentecost*, 1555

"When the day of Pentecost had come, they were all together in one place. And suddenly a sound came from heaven like the rush of a mighty wind, and it filled all the house where they were sitting. And there appeared to them tongues as of fire, distributed and resting on each one of them. And they were all filled with the Holy Spirit and began to speak in other tongues, as the Spirit gave them utterance" (*Acts* 2:1-4).

"'Holy Spirit' is the proper name of the one whom we adore and glorify with the Father and the Son. The Church has received this name from the Lord and professes it in the Baptism of her new children" (*CCC*, 691).

Tiziano Vecellio, *Our Lady assumed into Heaven*, 1518

THE ASSUMPTION

"Henceforth all generations will call me blessed; for he who is mighty has done great things for me" (*Lk* 1:48-49).

"The Most Blessed Virgin Mary, when the course of her earthly life was completed, was taken up body and soul into the glory of heaven, where she already shares in the glory of her Son's Resurrection, anticipating the resurrection of all members of his Body" (*CCC*, 974).

Pinturicchio, *The Crowning of the Blessed Virgin*, 1503

THE CROWNING OF OUR LADY QUEEN OF HEAVEN

"And a great portent appeared in heaven, a woman clothed with the sun, with the moon under her feet, and on her head a crown of twelve stars" (*Rev* 12:1).

"Finally the Immaculate Virgin, preserved free from all stain of original sin, when the course of her earthly life was finished, was taken up body and soul into heavenly glory, and exalted by the Lord as Queen over all things, so that she might be the more fully conformed to her Son, the Lord of lords and conqueror of sin and death" (*CCC*, 966).

Prayers

Jesus teaching the Our Father, 13th century, London

Our Father

Our Father,
who art in heaven,
hallowed be thy name,
thy kingdom come,
thy will be done
on earth
as it is in heaven.

Give us this day
our daily bread
and forgive us our trespasses
as we forgive those
who trespass against us,
and lead us not
into temptation
but deliver us from evil.
Amen.

HAIL MARY

Hail, Mary,
full of grace,
the Lord is with thee:
blessed art thou among
women,
and blessed is the fruit
of thy womb, Jesus.
Holy Mary,
Mother of God,
pray for us sinners,
now,
and at the hour of our death.
Amen.

Blessed Fra Angelico, *The Annunciation* (detail), 1440-52

GLORY BE TO FATHER

Glory be to the Father,
and to the Son,
and to the Holy Spirit.
As it was in the beginning,
is now, and ever shall be,
world without end.
Amen.

Andrej Rublev, *Trinity*, c. 1410

LITANY OF THE BLESSED VIRGIN

Lord have mercy.

Christ have mercy.

Lord have mercy.

Christ hear us.

Christ graciously hear us.

God, the Father of heaven,
have mercy on us.

God the Son, Redeemer of the world,

God the Holy Spirit,

Holy Trinity, one God,

Holy Mary,
pray for us.

Holy Mother of God,

Holy Virgin of virgins,

Mother of Christ,

Mother of the Church,

Mother of divine grace,

Mother most pure,

Mother most chaste,

Michelangelo Buonarotti, *Pietà* (detail), 1499

LITANY OF THE BLESSED VIRGIN

Mother inviolate,
Mother undefiled,
Mother most amiable,
Mother most admirable,
Mother of good counsel,
Mother of our Creator,
Mother of our Saviour,
Virgin most prudent,
Virgin most venerable,
Virgin most renowned,
Virgin most powerful,
Virgin most merciful,
Virgin most faithful,
Mirror of justice,
Seat of wisdom,
Cause of our joy,
Spiritual vessel,
Vessel of honour,
Singular vessel of devotion,
Mystical rose,
Tower of David,

Rogier Van der Weyden, *The Deposition*, c. 1435-40.

Tower of ivory,
House of gold,
Ark of the covenant,
Gate of heaven,
Morning star,
Health of the sick,
Refuge of sinners,
Comfort of the afflicted,
Help of Christians,
Queen of Angels,
Queen of Patriarchs,
Queen of Prophets,
Queen of Apostles,
Queen of Martyrs,
Queen of Confessors,
Queen of Virgins,
Queen of all Saints,

Queen conceived without original sin,
Queen assumed into heaven,
Queen of the most holy Rosary,
Queen of families,
Queen of peace.

Centro Aletti, *The Annunciation*, 1999

Lamb of God, who takest away the sins of the world,
spare us, O Lord.

Lamb of God, who takest away the sins of the world,
graciously hear us, O Lord.

Lamb of God, who takest away the sins of the world,
have mercy on us.

Pray for us, O holy Mother of God.
That we may be made worthy of the promises of Christ.

Let us pray.
Grant, we beseech thee,
O Lord God,
that we, your servants,
may enjoy perpetual health of mind and body;
and by the intercession of the Blessed Mary, ever Virgin,
may be delivered from present sorrow,
and obtain eternal joy.
Through Christ our Lord.
Amen.

Hail holy Queen

Hail, holy Queen,
mother of mercy;
hail, our life,
our sweetness and our hope.
To thee do we cry,
poor banished children of Eve;
to thee do we send up our sighs,
mourning and weeping in this
valley of tears.
Turn then, most gracious advocate,
thine eyes of mercy towards us;
and after this our exile,
show unto us the blessed fruit
of thy womb, Jesus.
O clement, O loving,
O sweet Virgin Mary.
Amen.

Piero della Francesca, *Madonna della Misericordia*, 1460 ca.

Table of contents

VATICAN PRESS